Wander

Collection of poetry and thoughts

by
Nataša Benedičič

While every precaution has been taken in the preparation of this book, the publisher assumes no responsibility for errors or omissions, or for damages resulting from the use of the information contained herein.

WANDERERS

First edition. November 6, 2023.

Copyright © 2023 Nataša Benedičič.

ISBN: 979-8223083603

Written by Nataša Benedičič.

Table of Contents

Poetry

Lines on your palms are lives
of generations born before you.
The paths taken, doors closed.
There are questions lingering
in the corridors of your mind.
Dreams have become skeletons
in the darkest corner of your closet.
The child in you weary
of waiting as the adult in you roams
this graveyard of forgotten
dreams. In you is an insatiable hunger
for adventure, to rejoice
in wide open spaces; yet you're caught
like a boat tied up in a harbour.
We're all born wanderers, always returning
back to the child we were.
Are we aware of the vastness that resides within us?

Poets' sleep

Before they pour down on these pages;
I strive to make my thoughts comprehensible.
Yet sleep captures me; into a dream I flee every time.
Silence – a familiar friend – accompanies
the feet of a wanderer.
Muse has been throwing rocks at my window
- broken glass lays scattered.
Showing skulls of people lost forever
- like my voice immersed in these poems;
Words captured - together forming skeletons of ideas;
Who will recite them and hear me?
Nonetheless, my journey through the fields
of imagination is a passion I don't question.
I will be returning to them
- until death infuses my flesh
and even after, my spirit wishes
to haunt these skeletons it created.

Stream of consciousness

note follows a note
like night follows day
rusty old piano
still ready to tell a tale
but I fear I don't know
the keys any more
what will we
achieve in this lifetime?
I wonder who will walk
behind me, trying to finish
all the ideas I failed to create
all the stories I failed to write
all the poems I kept inside
it's easy to judge the past
when looking at it from the future
how it steals us from the now
the long hours spent
being locked inside
your own shell
ever noticed what thoughts
became a part of you?
how some words
became a comfort zone?

some evenings it pours,
pours down in your mind,
the things that could've been
the moments you could've lived
leave a different taste of the days
maybe find a way to best describe –
the rhythm of the hearts you miss
the warmth of a loved one in your bed
the scent of your new-born in your hands
the way you felt happy when you
stretched the limits of your body and mind
the freedom you found when you acquired the void
the constant yearning to hear the music
and just dance in this universe
of possibilities and dreams

To find the human

Like a lost cloud in the sea of infinity,
with no connection to any place,
words trapped inside a bubble flow.
There are raging storms in this body of water;
waves rumble in the depths,
shaping the surface from the inside,
guarding pieces that have yet not been broken.
Constantly searching for the calm of rightfulness.
Poet stands on the bridge between this reality
and what lays beyond the horizon;
baffled by all the possibilities, extending
dimensions of imagination, to open the eyes
in a world gone blind.
Who does it take to hear the song
of the tales that have long been unsung?
How many layers do we wrap our lives in?
So we can present this picture-perfect scenario
to the eyes of the world,
but loose our own sense of humanity;
What nurtures our dreams?
Living simultaneously as a part in endless stories;
Where do we find a place
to find the human in us?

Treading in flood

I've been hiding in a tree
on a branch which understands sadness
I like the rain the most when it
gently kisses the skin
so the roots can grow peacefully
it takes time and wrong decisions to find home
a place where your heart will glow
lately, the rain came pouring down
and all I want to do is run,
run away
scream at the top of my lungs
as if another storm is coming
this time, coming from within
treading in flood I turn around and think
is this the life I'm supposed to be living?

Letting go

as I search for the house of sun
to perish the sorrows of the past
the wrong doings that took place
I realize that we will always be learners
we are what we think
our thoughts flow like fish
either with the current or against it
but until we learn to master them
we can use a flash light to mark the blame
or a magic wand to lose ourselves
beliefs build up our realities
they are so easily accessible
from a fountain to a telephone
the path can have many peaks
and descents; it may feel like
it will never change
but all is there for a reason
when you stop to let go
and accept yourself
the direction will also change

Silence has its ending

the times are bleak,
cold and always passing
yet sunlight comes creeping in
putting a light on the dust settled on the wings
of ideas you shaped, but never kept the fire burning
your body transformed into that one of a tin man
and now you know how it feels to bleed rust
the seeds you water will sprout
every leaf has possibilities and a purpose
even after it dies away
it merges with the soil and feeds
the new ones, preparing to bloom
every waiting,
like silence,
has its ending.

Simmering warmth

when did it become so hard to look at things
with innocent eyes of a child?
now you realize that growing up was more
harmful than they would dare admit to you
trusting in blind faith that the same choices
will bring new results is utopic
where do you find your haven
when you get scared to look inside of yourself?
as if you've become just a basket
for other peoples' instructions and opinions
it only works if it matters to you
million bulbs in the eyes turn on
when we speak of something
we're passionate about
whole night sky can be captured
in those moments when
we never felt more alive
inside it simmers
as if out of nothing it gives
no matter how cold it may get
no matter how the wind may roar
there's a warmth inside spreading
like electricity through our bodies

and it usually sparks just when you've
almost ready to give up
the most rewarding thing about it is
that it can be shared
and then it can spread like wild fire
and feels twice as good

Every leaf is a thought

every leaf is a thought
that falls
from the mouth,
touching the ground
some yellow,
some red with fire
they either mark the new path
or soil the old one;
they can carry
different weight,
although logically
they are all the same,
made of letters
and words; yet some
fall heavy on the heart
and can weight a person down,
some touch the heart gently
and they lift up the spirit, as if
they attached a balloon on it
it takes the same amount of time
and energy,
but the intention
has different arrows and aims;

fear is a powerful tool,
it spreads like wild fire,
burning bridges;
through the smoke
we stay blind to the truth,
as the war over power rages on
and you will never know
the amount of hearts in need of mending
and what will it take to fix it all

Deep inside

you can't recall the moment is starts
how it becomes like a haven you always searched for
somewhere away from those who can't relate
building yourself through these miniature storms
until nothing else feels like home
you only realize the strange comfort if brings
and how often you dive into it,
like it's the air you breathe
familiar waves surrounding your thoughts
but you don't feel the sadness that clings to your lungs
becoming your second skin
let the storms pass,
before they take you
like the ocean,
you too can calm yourself

About time

Time should be a logical thing
made up of dates, hours, minutes, seconds...
one following the other, same measure – anyway you look at it
It may have happened a year ago,
but it seems as if it was yesterday
It may have happened a few months ago,
but it seems as if it was few years ago
as if our internal clocks go as they please
with a mind of their own
such a relative thing, yet it controls
much of our thinking and planning
It has many expectations – what
we expect to have and achieve to a certain age
not questioning if we are ready
but searching for a perfect time
also has its flaws
Do you know how many hours you spent sleeping?
And how dreams bend that perception of time?
And how hard it is on some days, to just get out of bed
How many dreams have you dreamt
from the worst nightmare
to the feelings you could only dream up?
so many problems you resolved

14

as you drifted away
from the stairs of the past
from the promise of the future
time has the ability to cure many woes
you live in a maze of space and time
and all you have is now
everything else is a distraction
we all yearn for the moments
when time just stops and stands still
like when you look into your lovers eyes
and there is just the two of you in the universe

Dreamers

under the light of the universe
a rainbow extends between the rose
I carry in my arms and the rest
of my wishes in the wishing well
deep in my dreams I am alone
being swept under the golden
and yellow leaves through the mists
of what hides behind the next step
you find me gazing at the moon
and I wonder why it's so simple
to fall into you - the touch of your fingers
runs through the depths of my skin
setting fire to all the things I thought
I knew to be true
shadows disappear
as we collide
into each others' eyes
time has a way of bringing
our dreams down
and in this world rich
are the dreamers
and I hope ours' get to shine

In between moments

waking up from sleep at 4 pm
thoughts hazy and black
can't put a finger on how long I've been away
feels like coming back from the edge of life
pushing me out to do what matters most
there's a sadness all my own
can't explain how lonely it can get
how can we put time linearly
when measuring it feels like
putting it into a cup
some days seem to never end
and others they just fly us by
some moments stay close
and others go down in history
all in all, it's one big mixed cloud of the past
there's a beat coming from the earth
like warm, slow waves of the sea
embracing and calling us in
time is like grains of sand
slowly vanishing into memories
when you walk through
the forest of your reminiscence
you realize the importance

of choosing the people you live with
how they colour your days
different imprints they leave in the heart
most decisions made are based on the feeling in the eyes
- how they steal
and give
and always speak the truth
how you think about yourself
makes all the difference
the way you carry your soul
either you lift it up to find home
or you suppress it from growing
night driving - miles rolling by
freshly you pick up where you left off
as you choose the next destination
and search for something better
hoping all this would change
soul finds home somewhere in between those miles
those long and heartwarming seconds
that we carry till the ends of the earth
and are only ours to know and experience
leaving a smile on our faces

Wanderers

There have been many dark valleys
and tunnels your soul has endured
It roamed around unknown places
for so long, even crows knew your name
Deep inside, you always knew
which road was meant for you
Many fights and obstacles you fought
and no one can answer, how many more await
Some days all you do is look for meaning
in every *"why?"* and *"what for?"*
Remember bad choices, until you learn from them
then let them go,
learn to let things go
There is no guarantee for what follows next
it's a game, where it's hard to speak
of degrees of fairness
Some things depend on each other
and you can't have one thing without the other
but in order to leave that point, you need it,
but you can't get it because you haven't yet left
Everything is in constant motion
- f l o w i n g, and time can change every-<u>thing</u>
even your s k i n

You speak of TIME as a thing of the past; or of the future
and in how much you still have it, or how much you don't
but you fail to see it has enslaved you from the moment.
You are an explorer,
always on an adventure
striving to reach that perfect space
holding life in the highest regard
it's an amazing thing, how it survives
no matter the odds
You realize you have much more ***to learn***
and much more ***to give***; you feel the seeds
of ideas in your mind, not yet ready to burst
Through your own eyes you discover laws
on which this world is made upon
Inside you're full of bruises that are hidden
to the naked eye; yet they are as much a part of you
as your heart will ever be; you'll never know
the scent you leave behind
Are you even aware of the vastness
that resides within you?
Yet you seek external stimulus,
to distract you from being true and free
For *what would other people think?*
We like to think we're winners
Many great civilizations fell before us
and we failed to learn from history
We arrive
and we leave
So be true in your intentions
and take care of the Earth,

for it sustains life
in many wondrous forms.
Find your balance
- in anything you do
Find a companion
with a gentle heart
Find your voice
and be brave enough
to speak it clearly.
Take a breath
and look up to the sky
and search for stars
Among it, you will find
a place where you belong

Autumn in Madeira

when autumn wind blows
and brings with it that familiar scent
I pack my bags and move to my tree house
in the shelter of tree trunks I create
a village where my soul becomes alive again
I put my thoughts on the leaves
and watch them disappear
for everything that is, perishes
I know the world to be written in tragedies
but beauty of life shines through them
in all the seconds we get
we can guess which one will be our last
which one will bring change
and in which one we will get lost
but in one second your life can pass you by
and it's up to you what you made out of it
divide your days into the things
your heart believes in
and observe it grow
do we allow to be happy and just to be?
and do we let others grow
do we speak in a matter that allows
roses to still grow as roses?

Human maps

feeling of comfort flows over
as I hug my legs, and pulling
the weary knees closer to the heart,
like a foetus, comfortably floating and not
demanding anything, funny how we litter
our minds with things, how we surround our skins,
pushing us further away from nature,
how we expose our bare skin, but hide
our hearts, as if it takes a miracle
to find love, gently the curls tickle
the skin, playfully reminding the magic
the body can sense, so many skins we shed
in process of developing the current
personality, yet it's hard to put a finger on
what stayed the same, strange to imagine,
it only took two cells to start building a body,
what do you call a mistake?
our skins, a perfect map
and we love the person
who lovingly discovers
all the bruises, valleys and gaps
and still sees the perfection of the being within

Who we are on the inside

when and where do you begin to be?
we count the weeks, then months, then years
but it started way before in secret, in thought
two cells collided and before you know it
a new heart started beating
how do you measure up your life?
in years? in months? in weeks?
we all live in the same now, but our realities
are so very different, living through days
and taking tomorrows for granted
everything you feel now you carry into the future
when it can feel like it just happened, sower of time we are
reliving the past as if it's present
carrying the load for years before you start asking
whose is it?
our stories are our, we are the writers
we don't need anyone to tell us who to be
yet we feel burdened to be what others say
we should be, although most people listen
just to reply
how can we feel separated from nature?
we may feel like we don't belong here
our instincts shut, our senses dulled

feeling the hollowness inside
wanting our lives to have meaning
born into the system, we learn and we adapt
so eager to grow up, we forget how to paint and play
we are just like the air, fire, water, earth IS
not separate, but one,
for we are nature
why do we close ourselves inside?
attach to things that keep us forever occupied
we have no time for ourselves
we all know something needs to be done,
but we're so comfortable in our glitter
when do we allow our lungs just to breathe fully?
we lost connection to everything that actually matters
burning the ground underneath as we go
are our lives but shadows,
a mere reflection of an echo
who are we, roaming these wastelands?
a shooting star in the earths existence?
the emotions we feel are vast to us
the journeys we make are our own
who are we on the inside?
- the whole universe?
maybe it's enough to know
who we are not

Love of thousands

the heart can stumble, fall, float or drown in silence
the mind flying behind it, tries to reason with it
offering compromises in last rational attempts
and then the echo of a storm is seen in the eyes
but dive far enough, there will be peace,
there will be love
you carry love of thousands inside you
all your ancestors fought against the odds
took chances, met coincidences, played with fate
engaged in the game of love, ignited fires
into new hearts, exchanged stardust on the fingertips
with those they touched
they are long hidden in the corners of your cells
somehow they still live on inside your name
as you stand here now, lost in a small memory
of the journey behind how your heart started beating
what does it take for two souls to meet?

At the edge of the ocean

At the edge of the ocean
I heard you call my name
Felt you in my bones
That's how deeply entwined
our souls have become through the ages
A time forgotten has come back
as we start to remember
the songs we used to sing
as we were playing together
running our fingertips
throughout each others' lives
so distant yet so near
Gently we remind one another
of the path we chose.

Gap between the breaths

whoever will get to taste my bones
and discover my highway full of secrets
there is an everlasting light which haunts me
in dreams I disappear completely to a place
where starlight kisses the sky
it ignites my skin for it knows my voice
stories wrapped in melody
in the gap between the breaths
songs are like bells calling us home
we ask ourselves hard questions
looking for answers our whole lives
in this wretched sea of denial
passion leads words to freedom
I am the ocean, a river of thoughts
flowing through the flesh
there are rooms with different versions
of our selves, various landscapes
through which we fought on our adventures
memories are like creatures
sneaking up on you in the middle of a sentence
the ones you feed, will gladly come back for more
and change their shape to fit in
others, they fade to black

sitting in silence until forgotten
unless they scheme to fill the melody
in the gap between the breaths

Houses breathe us in

houses breathe us in
their walls dripping with time past, entwine lifelines
the museums of our triumphs, failures and milestones
all filled with stains from which we grew
places we've been to are wired like electrons to our memories
returning, revisiting at any moment
from the forests where the battles of history unfolded
to the mists of the April rain showers
and the sunlight of the evening catching your desires
you were there,
that's why it matters
a certain feeling, a sound - like a silk tread
pierces through our hearts, evoking a traveller within

Welcome to the dream

From a speck you unfold like the universe
what is it that you take as a part of your essence?
The picture we send out to the world
can easily distort itself, the mirror shatters
In the darkest of nights and in the brightest of days
do you remain the same? True to what you believe?
Do you feel the core of your being unchanged?
Out of the million possibilities of who you could've been
you are who you are due to chance? Or some greater plan?
After everything that matters to you, has been taken away
can you still paint the sky a bright colour as a child?
Can you guess the cards you've been dealt?
When does it happen, can you tell, when your eyes become blind?
The heart singing in silence is the saddest sound,
- like the ocean slowly weeping
Voice boxes with nothing to say, but sell your humanity
How long can you run with your wounds unintended?
Hiding scars in all sorts of unexpected places.
I found the creature who would lick my wounds
deep in the forest of my own thoughts.

Things you said under the stars

We've fought battles
hand in hand
We've stood the test of time
victorious
Our eyes are full of dreams
and wonder
Can you feel your skin
calling to life;
as we gaze up the night sky trying to
decipher
the language of stars -
our home
so distant and unknown;
as if we can't
find it in our eyes.

This world is our playground

Wood creaks in the wind,
the cold sweeping
through the walls
blazing sun rays
painting the evening skies.
All the places your mind
wanders to in dreams,
staying with you like a reality
you once lived through.
All the scenarios you feed your mind;
unknowingly you change
the colours of your everyday emotions.
How much does the shadow weight?
Does it drag you down on the floor –
or does it lift you up?
What kind of messages did you store
when you were young?
What went through your head -
as you were searching
for that person you should be
as if the community knew,
as if it was written
somewhere for you to follow.

When all along, it has only been written in you.
Then you come to realize the freedom,
which at some point,
might have suffocated your mind.
You can't outrun
what happened; it follows you.
Which path you choose
is only up to you to decide.
There are two worlds -
we chase each other through.
One in which we act as mirrors
and walk towards whatever satisfies us.
Second, where we get lost
in reflections of the first one
in our minds.
And whatever we do, we die twice.
This world is our playground,
leave something meaningful,
make a change,
before you exit.

Years weigh differently in the heart

fiery surface of the river shining against the blue sky
golden pathway leading through the forests
- dressed in the autumn cloak
you may not notice it at first, but mirrors disappear
in the light of the nature at its finest
shadows of buildings haunting the dawning of the day
and I keep on singing the old familiar song about loneliness
lyrics lay on the tip of my tongue, can taste it in a kiss
our history is soaked through and through with blood spilled
yet the oceans remain deep blue and green
of today's blood maybe the next generations will speak
they will be the judge of the fools we've been
it's up to them to select the books they will believe
much remains unwritten and unsaid
death still scares us, we keep distancing ourselves from it
until it reaches somewhere close to our hearts
how many days do we have to spend
before they are worth something to us?
how do you count the years
when they weigh differently in your heart?
we prefer to value something when we start to lose it
how many paths will we discover
before we find the right purpose of our lives

and decide it's time to follow it
will we ever achieve everything we set our minds to do
or are we just chasing those shadows
of dreams long gone, the ideas
that keep on slipping away
soaked with tears and sweat
how long before you know the role
you were meant to play?
maybe the one you never would have signed for
can you still recall the feelings
of all the masks you threw away
having learned everything or nothing at all
striving to keep the picture together
the over-valued science of being busy,
successful, yet poor in original thought
in the long run, the question is
which memories matter most?

Sand of time

How many times has a part of you died
for a new one to be born
Your body constantly repairing
and growing throughout your lifetime
Yet it hides behind the same name,
the same I
How many times have you stood,
naked in words with someone, who later vanished
How many times have you stood
in complete silence with someone
and understood it all
Love that you feel is timeless
Path of growing and learning
is never ending
Healing your childhood wounds
by yourself as an adult
Changing your road and discovering
the secrets your mind plays
Ghosts of past, present and future
will haunt you
You'll learn to master the ship
as you sail through the time you have
Be doubtful of expectations,

they tend to make you bleed
Your words and actions
hold an immeasurable weight
Your footprints echo
in the valleys of time
Everything is woven into a spiral,
moving ever forward
Story changes colour,
depending from where you're observing
Beginning and ending
hold a much different picture
Just as the water permeates through
the sand grain, your why appears

Call to life

it seems ridiculous to count the time
when no matter how much time passes
it still feels like some people never left
holding the same essence of home
within your heart
now I know we're not the same people
as we were when we went into this storm
heavy darkness filled our lungs, questioning our minds
the world isn't what is seems
it won't always be this way
but I recall a time when we were free,
when no challenge was too big,
nothing could break our spirits
when we could stand and fall together
what do we worship now?
do we ever question what we had?
and for what did we exchange it?
maybe in another life we could
meet and have it all
maybe in some other world we do
where have we hidden the key
to the cage where our hearts are locked in?
are we but shadows roaming these streets?

love is nothing but a word we fool ourselves we know
until we honestly look ourselves in the mirror
Love is all there is, the only magic you need
it starts within you and if you water it, it grows
let your heart be vulnerable, it's stronger than you think
let yourself feel the feelings and don't close the doors
we were born and we will die, in between we're alive
you're here to find out what that means for you
and life is calling you home

Lifetime Warriors

We're multilayered. Like a colourful woolen sweatshirt.
Not everyone can see, how many layers we carry -
for we hide behind them like a shield.
Since we know the world can be a lone, hard and cold place -
we hide for fear of being seen. We fear that people
will get to know us and abuse us for their own purpose.
Most of all - we fear being hurt.
We express ourselves through words and deeds;
Still there is much being unsaid, which only flickers
somewhere in the distance - inside our eyes.
We find comfort looking at the night sky,
because answers wait there for us.
There is a lot of difference between every hello & goodbye.
The one that comes last, always hits the hardest.
Regrets of things undone sweep in - they can fill a book.
Here and there life reminds us of the true purpose.
We're still discovering ourselves,
the multitudes that surround us;
Searching for meaning of our lives,
between the work that we do
and the bills we have to pay,
and the things we wish we were doing
or wish we'd had.

All the things we're so afraid to do and to be -
afraid to love,
afraid to be fragile,
afraid to show our skins,
afraid to shed our masks,
seems so minor and foolish when you stare into the abyss.
We shouldn't love for a reason, when the reason disappears, so
does the love.
We're chasing each other through the plains of stardust
time does not exist there.
Deep inside we know who we are and where we come from -
we make arrangements of the parts and lessons we will give
each other.
Not really knowing how it will feel, the path we will endure.
When our hearts collide together it feels like jumping into the
fountain of peace.
There is something so familiar when skin touches another skin.
We're warriors, and we roam these endless fields,
writing our stories. Each and every one unique. In it,
we're never alone. Touching and crashing into each other.
Lifetime, seems a fleeting moment. No one can really die,
if they stay in our hearts.

Dancer in the dark

you're a dancer in the dark
not knowing what and who you will become
floating in the ocean like an astronaut
pieces of stardust flowing through your blood
of a story that started long before knowing
like ripping out a page, burning it to dust
and let wind to take its meaning
what you're here to endure will be revealed along the path
we're here to hold our sadness to each his own
but may you not follow what others will lay out for you
may you look yourself in the mirror and recognize
your true self looking back at you
others will force their expectations upon you
and deep inside you'll know you won't be able to achieve them
being contradictory and ever-changing
which may leave you confused and wishing for something
to fit into an idea not yours
the thing is though, most people have no idea
leading a safe life in order to survive
don't be busy with living or days will pass you by
leave you empty yearning for something more
don't force too much of yourself, or if you do, ignite!
dive into the flame and keep it burning

Change

we are innocently born to this playground
mostly water, but not liquid, made from milk
admiring the bright yellow sun
where we find our freedom
voice speaking inside, without a mouth
we're learning who we are
the story behind a name unravels
songs begging to be felt, to be written
what was placed upon your shoulders?
parts of us crack open
like a cloud when it starts raining
some days you wish it would rain hope
hope in a form of seeds, so it would grow
we wish we could dance instead of race
where have we lost ourselves on the path?
mind weary from repeating the same maze
hungry for change - let it rise up from the ashes
let it flow through our lives
we've been lost and thirsty
pouring our cups with dreams
heart throbbing with yearning
what it could be like, asking for courage
to make a step in the right direction

44

what awaits there?

Will you know how to touch?

The reflections you leave of yourself
Are unique to the watchers themselves
The image you seek is out of your hands
The world an illusion to comprehend
Your body swimming in the melody of the heart
Time slows and speeds, every thought, every emotion stays
Either it builds up or it flows onwards
The pictures are yours to cherish
Your soul searching for the meaning of words
Hearing what is said in between or not at all
Your heart reaching for pieces of itself in various ways
Always yearning for a feeling of home, wherever and whatever
that may be
Life isn't a series of expected and anticipated events
You'll get lost in where you never knew you could get lost in
You'll be thrown in the water, but if you find your calm
You'll see you knew how to swim all along
Monsters in the closet will drag you down
But you'll learn that fear is there to overcome it
You may recite all words of wisdom, but they are worth
nothing
If you can't implement them in your life
Your life like a dream will vanish into thin air

Feed your curiosity, may the path lead you where it will
Unlock the strength of spirit hidden inside
Explore the space in which we exist
Love, above all, love; love yourself first,
Words are not enough, but they are a note of the piano key
That lets all the wild things of the heart loose
Eyes are the place where magic begins
Take care of the land around you,
deep in the forest are lessons waiting for you
You're not separate, you're one with it, with everyone around
you
Touch gently but firmly, naturally.

Cracking the shell

in the depth of the night
when sleep won't come
you feel oozing from the forgotten wounds
the need to fit in
and not stand out
not allowed to think
and feel differently
changing our faces
as we see fit
you grew
but with a lack of sun
you live
but still miss something
you hug your bones close
and think: "Look how far we've come."
calming the storms within
you keep on running through
these snow covered paths
leading through the forests
where old trees dwell
reaching the heights
and you can smell
the wisdom of the roots

you surrender to the pace
trusting the clarity it brings
you've lost parts of yourself
and you have found parts of yourself
they were always there
patiently waiting
have you found where your place is?
always rushing to fulfill your goals
always racing to get to the place unknown
roaming through darkest of clouds
what is it that haunts you?
why not just stop and let it find you?
born into this strange place
we search to solve the mysteries
the echo of your days
will fill your life
with whatever you give power to
you survived the storms
you never thought you would
our time here is limited
leave behind regrets
they are nothing but lessons
of your past decisions
it's all connected somehow
you've mended your broken bones
and sewn your heart and filled it with love
you will never know how long
your words and actions
linger in the minds of others
hopefully, warming their hearts

Full circle

To the person we once were
To the homes we've changed
To the one's we left behind
To the nights the moon was a savior
To the days we were broken
To the heart that wouldn't give in
To the times you felt trapped with no way out
To the days when no one understood you
To the moments you wish to store
To the endings and new beginnings
To the games we played
To the paths we ran
To the people who touched your heart
To the hardships we endured
To the changes we achieved
To the tears shed and laughs given
To the wisdom of the body
In the end it all comes up full circle,
light and darkness, into a picture of remembrance.
Your life one long journey of discovering oneself.

Life is heart-breaking

How long can you stare at the picture you painted,
blindfolded, believing it to be true? Everything
crumbles at your feet, as you walk in silence,
'cause no one is listening.
Every moment you ever lived,
every tear, every laugh, every
heart-breaking moment, every
soulful hour... everything passes
like sand through your hourglass.
Navigating through thick fog,
minutes before the day opens,
trees breathing silently.
We all carry scars inside,
where they remain unseen.
We all go through things
we can't talk about.
In a war, neither side wins.
With enough self-love,
does the scar tissue disappear?

Into the storm

We climb mountains of fear
and swim rivers of grief
Inner demons we fight
Boat is our heart
mind the captain
navigating through
the forest of wisdom
The thoughts of your past
are weighting you down
Body holding memories
When it starts to burn
at the staircase of your heart
Everything will start to gain new meaning
Restless soul
trapped in your own thinking
can't follow the rhythm of the heart
feeling the distant abandonment
of the life we wished we lived
We don't carve with chisel and hammer
but with thoughts and feelings
Lets heal the wounds
that bled for generations
into the earth, which

52

we all call home.

Sleeping giants

The miles
- they disappear in the rear view mirror
I hear
- the constant struggle of raindrops carving their way back home
The flame
- of my heart soaring to new heights
I hear
- the birds chirping at the start of the new dawn
My mortal voice gets lost among the sea waves
We don't feel that we are growing
Sleeping giants with amnesia
born with no promises of how life should be
or of what you should achieve
and by what age you should have achieved it by
it's all man made pressure
You can't hurry healing
Souls sharing time and space
tomorrows and yesterdays
in between we yearn for a deeper purpose
of our fleeting lives
getting lost in the importance of the flesh
forgetting our littleness

54

- in the cosmic play
our lives are like grains of sand.

For you

- who is tired of this in-between space
believe in yourself
remember it takes time to grow
life is a journey
of constantly searching
for our selves
for our purpose
the path might feel like the right one
yet you may still question your choice
look back, only to see how far you've come
if you ponder on peoples' opinions
you give them weight
it's just a reflection of themselves
you don't know how many times
your heart will be shattered into small pieces
- remember,
it's ALL temporary.

Let it.

But what if it burns?
Let it.
Let it burn the shell in which you are wrapped,
Let it burn through the chamber of your heart,
Let it tear down the walls, which hide you inside,
Let it clench your soul at the center,
Let it show you the darkness that has consumed you,
Let it burn away your old dreams,
Let it smoke out the shadows behind which you've been hidden,
Let it all take place,
And return into the new dawn,
You are stronger than you think.

Lost at sea

we're gazing at each other over the sea
looking at the rippled reflection we leave behind
draw me a map of your wounds and bruises
let's kiss each others scars
the life we live
is the shadow we leave behind
all the yesterdays,
all the tomorrows
are rooted inside you,
into your experience of I
we tell our stories in our own voice
our heartbeat is written into the soil
our hands touch
and our reflections merge into one
I dive into the water, homesick,
I will wait for you there.

I know the sound of your heart

you're in my blood
like a long forgotten memory
of the time your body was
developing under my heart
your arms and legs moved
gently, in the darkness of the womb
listening to the sounds my body made
our cells are intertwined for eternity
I knew the sound of your heart,
(as you knew mine)
even before you were born
your chest on my chest
rhythm of our hearts guiding us home

Heartbeat

Our eyes are timeless,
the universe looking back at itself,
wordlessly.
Hold your gaze a little longer,
everything can change
in a blink of an eye.
Years and the days we lived,
our paths cross again and again.
Stand close to me, heart to heart,
where we seemed to be tied.
Let me run my fingertips over your
neck and chest, and meet your heartbeat.
Nothing stays, but this lingering feeling,
of a distant home, so close I could taste it.

Torchbearer

When I think I've reached the bottom,
you show me new depths of love,
as if it's an endless well,
and your voice echoes inside.
Unintentionally, we touch each other
in a million ways; your road is yours to walk,
and I admire your actions and decisions.
There is freedom in finding ourselves,
our life is ours to live, courageous are those
who can just be and know themselves.
I was rushing for a future self,
but you taught me life is not to be rushed.
Everything is as it should be.
Surrender to the quiet,
what you feel is yours.

Beautiful scars

There is so much beauty -
in the strength it took you to stand up,
to show love for yourself,
even though you never received it
to be gentle, even though
you've never been shown much kindness
to hold me close, even though
you were never held close as a child.
People sure love in strange and different ways.
We're two people who could clearly see each other,
but were never seen for who they truly are.

Endless possibilities

My head under water,
browsing through my thoughts,
or so I think, they are mine.
Somewhere, when things get
quiet, I can hear the beating
of a drum, the rhythm
so indistinctly mine.
Birds flying, leaving no
trace behind, on the deep
blue canvas. Inside of us
are endless stories, some
happy, some sad, yet
infinitely ours. Inside of us
are endless possibilities,
no matter how broken
we've become.

I taught myself

I taught myself
how to stand still
while the ocean roars inside
I taught myself
to never reveal everything
for fear of not fitting in
I taught myself
there is beauty
in being who you really are
I taught myself
how to tend to my wounds
for in life you have to take care of yourself
I taught myself
to be stubborn
otherwise my goals will just laugh at me
I taught myself
to think it over
before speaking up
through it all... I never taught myself
how to stand in the light
how to raise my voice not to be shut down
how to spend the time that has been given to me
so that when the time is up, I won't have any regrets.

I admit

I admit
the intensity took me by surprise
- perpetually unprepared
how at first you can't seem to breathe,
can't seem to run as fast as you should,
and how the heart aches at first,
but then it eases and expands.
I admit
it was selfish of me to think,
my heart will always be just mine,
when in fact it can burst open,
and grow inside the bodies of others,
feeling a person so close, but they are far away,
yet they remain in a corner of your heart.
I admit
to falsely believing
we can control our emotions,
when in fact we only control how we handle them,
as if they are some kind of an exercise,
on how much our heart muscles can bear.
I admit
love grows, if you let it.

The act of leaving

it's not that I've fallen,
but I feel stuck, as if
I've fallen down the fountain,
and my friends are just
echoes of ghosts in the walls
it's not that I've drowned,
but I feel as if, I'm drowning
somewhere deeper into the depths
of the dark hues of the ocean
and I'm neither heard nor seen
it's not that I've failed,
but I don't seem to understand
the game they are playing
as if we're actors in a masquerade
and I don't want to play my part
it's not that I am eager to leave,
but I don't want to be
living like this any longer
we're all growing, and sometimes
it feels as if we outgrow the space we are in

Some people

Some people are like acorns,
they fall into the unknown grounds,
and with little sunshine and a little rain,
they sprout, without knowing how,
they grow tall and are a signpost for others,
offering a safe haven in the shades.
Some people look at you,
as if they have stars in their eyes,
milky way at their feet, their thoughts
are echoes of the cosmic winds,
touching you deeply and profoundly,
gently guiding others across the night sky.
Some people have a fire in their hearts,
that no amount of water can put out,
it rages with a passion known only to them,
they burn their bridges and their cords,
from out of that smoke a phoenix rises,
again and again, for they are unstoppable.
Some people are a little lost at sea,
soaked by rain, searching for a current,
constantly plunging from a stream to a waterfall,
the secrets of the deep blue ocean are
written in their bones, maybe that's why,

they are a bit restless, always searching for home.

Echos of the past

Memories are echos of the past in your mind,
Captivating you from the present moment,
They give your days a certain weight,
Your heart racing, your breathing heavy,
When you repeat certain past emotion.
A moment of what will come next, what will happen to you,
Carrying the weight of the world on our shoulders,
Roaming around, watching where you're stepping,
Days living on autopilot, as if you're willingly caged,
What does it take to lessen
the seriousness of our fleeting existence?
Why do we extinguish
the passion of our wide-eyed children?
Do not silence the child within you,
he is only asking to be heard
and loved unconditionally.

Dandelion dreams

She couldn't calm her mind easily. Even as a child,
her imagination roamed on long legs; and her mind
hardly kept up with the stories she spoke. Soft and
fragile, yet strong willed she danced through the days.
Chasing her dreams, which flew with the wind, like
dandelion seeds. Guarding her untamed heart,
healing it every time it broke. Staying true to
herself, not letting others sway her thoughts.
I hope your dandelion dreams get to shine bright,
on the big blue sky; I hope to find you there.

The space between our hearts

Whenever our eyes met, I saw fire burning in your eyes,
the one which you usually dim for others. When I stood
close to you, I felt as if strings from your heart were opening
up mine; as if you're opening a book, not to read or write
a chapter, but to make me see me in a mirror, which is you.
Our bodies are carrying cracks – the moonlight shines
through them. We glow ever so differently under ever-lasting
light of the universe. Yet there is something familiar
that connects us. The very cells of our hearts. The
timeless journey of atoms circling in our bloodstream.
The space between our hearts
intangible.

Your shutter is a window to the past

Memories reside in your mind,
how tangible do they seem?
There is a constancy you feel to
your character; day to day
you don't seem to change,
yet when years accumulate
you look at yourself and
question who you have become?
The cells that make your body
have all been replaced several
times in your lifetime. The proof
is there in the photographs
you look at; your shutter is a
window to the past – connecting
you to the moments that may have
gotten lost in the room of your mind.

Novaturient

When you do what is expected,
but that doesn't fill your soul.
You put your foot, one
in front of the other, following
that desire. Do you have the
answer to the question:
"What is it that I need?"
When you're always waiting,
always searching a way
to escape this moment.
Brokenly looking for a sign
to find your way.
You're like a stream train
running, but is this path
truly yours? When your soul
is eager to master the blowing wind
and the raging seas.
Your years forming a petal
rose and they transform
into butterflies.

Stain glass castles

April rain pouring down with thunder,
caught at a red light; few notes on the radio
and you're transported into the endless
and careless summer days you've had
as a child. Roaming the forests
and meadows in solitude.
You dealt with things as you knew how,
nobody there to hold your hand;
People came and went,
like passengers on the train.
With memories we built
stain glass castles through which
we'll be looking our whole life.
The colourful shades shadowing
our adult days. Only once
do we walk the path of childhood.
Yet we can revisit anytime;
Peace comes with accepting.

Anchored in silence

I stand before the book of dreams.
My voice anchored in silence,
much like a tree breathing in winter.
My fingers rusty and hard as they
brush over the pages. Solitude
surrounding me like a shadow.
My heart like a lost vagabond
wandering from a dream to a dream.
Even in darkness seeking a ray -
an inner light which guides me.
It's a journey of the unknown terrain
and unknown events. Given the only
instructions: "Feed with love."

Explore the hidden caves

We're all just children of the universe. When I say just,
I don't mean to belittle the role. There is stardust
running through our veins. Our mind a galaxy of wonders.
Yet we're so caught in the stagnant beliefs and standards
of living we think we need. Our bodies grow up,
and we abandon the spirit of the child living within;
yearning to play, sing, discover, jump, climb,
dance, create... who told you to leave that joy behind,
to hide your true beauty, to diminish your light?
And to exchange it for what?
There is endless power within you,
to relive your past and rewrite
your emotional signature. To heal
and be stronger than before; to let
the light shine through the cracks;
to explore the hidden caves of your
own heart, for you don't know
the depths of it; to feel all the colours
that reside in there; to let go
of your demons and let
the butterflies loose... and breathe
the future in.

I exhale

I exhale in the dark blue,
listening to the song of the wind,
my heart pounding with emotions,
air bears the wisdom of the forest,
of giants and dragons sleeping;
Moon quietly gazing at her
reflection on the surface of the water.
Sadness dripping in my veins,
I've swam in it for years,
it lingers even in my voice.
I inhale the freshness
and ask myself: "If not here, than where?"
It's not written in any book,
nor can any body else know,
it is inside of me, and out there
for me to find out. There is a red
thread connecting all of my days.
I may not know where it leads,
I may have lost my inner compass,
I may have walked a path that was not mine.
I can smell the magic
which brought me here.

Paint the sky

She is trying to describe a thought
without using words. The images
she sees are like pools in which
she swims. Belonging only to her.
Never experienced youth, always
felt older than her age. Outsider
in the roles she got. Her heart
is a forest of colourful trees,
every ring on the trunk carries
a short story of a life lived.
Our sense of who we are
is lost in our illusions
of what we think we should be,
what we think other people
expect us to be. Should we wake,
uncover our blindfolds, and open
our hearts to the person we are.
And paint the sky with our fingertips.

Homesick heart

Memories slip through your mind, like a movie clip,
the misty morning fog, the dew on the glass-blade
shining in the morning sun, the colourful leaves
flying in the air, catching snowflakes with the tip
of your tongue, hearing voices whispering
through the wind, the flutter of birds wings,
your bare feet touching the soil, walking tall,
belonging to this earths' matter. Then one day
you wake up, sorrow lingering in your voice,
why do you feel you're not enough? What
are you chasing so hard it won't let you breathe?
Stop. Wrap your arms around your chest. Feel
the force behind your beating heart. Give
yourself everything you need, to find that child
you left behind, he's still there, the same heart
beating in your rib cage, eager to come home
to himself.

How to heal these wounds?

There are doors you wish to never open.
There a paths you wish never to walk.
It's been raining inside of your heart.
Darkness of your days consuming your thoughts.
You've been a prisoner of your own silence.
You whisper into the dead of the night:
"How to heal these wounds?"
Unwrap and unfold, let go of what
you've been holding on to.
Do you know the courage of turning a page
and letting go of all that you knew?
When you walk down the crossroads,
wondering which path is yours to take,
remember our lives flow like a river.
It hurts because it matters.

Firefly

There is a universe inside of you,
a map of roots and vessels,
the magic that build your bones
still resides at the root of your deepest self;
You needed no one but yourself.
Stardust in your fingertips
dances when you touch someone.
Breathe in the language of the wind,
whispering the ancient melody.
We distance ourselves from
the growing pains we experienced as children.
When the fragments of your mind
become unknown to you,
I hope you get to see the light
shining through you; may your soul
light your path like a firefly.

Accidental soulmates

What brings two people together,
going their own way, wandering,
not searching for someone, yet
they find each other eye to eye
and they feel as if they were
meant to meet at this time.
As if they continue the story
where they ended in a distant time.
Diving deeper into the meaning of it all;
it's easy to forget yourself.
This time around, what will
remain unwritten and what words
will still remain unspoken?

The trees we sow

We are the trees our parents sown.
Elders walking through the forest
question it, yet they helped it grow.
We learn from each other, our roots
entwined. Each different, yet the same;
writing its story in the sand of time.
You can experience this life only
through your own narrative. But
in this life, no matter how brief
or long, you hold immense power,
unbeknownst to you. It may sound
too simple. Show love. Love strengthens,
love heals, love spreads deep
into the roots. Watch how little
it takes for trees to flourish.

Thoughts

*

She said: "Don't take life so seriously.
And I smiled, because a weight has been lifted."

*

Texture of hope
It burns like a small star in the night sky.
It warms you like a small candle warms the room.
Even if it starts small, it can spread to ENCOURAGE,
giving you something to hold on to, while
you're fighting your darkness.

*

Silent warriors we are
fighting with the power of words
in a world that has forgotten how to listen

*

Show me the world
inside your truest self.

*

I've been running for so long,
I've forgotten how to dance.

*

When was the last time you looked at the stars
and dived into that feeling

*

It's old and it runs deep
I can feel it in my bones
some people just feel like home
and stay with you for life
be they present or not
We all but speak one language.

*

Whilst you still have time to dream, dream big.
Leave behind what no longer feels right.
Let your spark ignite hope.
Be the magician in your story.
You're far greater than you think.

*

What if instead
of looking for flaws
we looked for virtue
and strength,
the unique beauty
of expression of life.

*

The longest relationship you'll ever have
is with that voice inside your head.
Don't let it drown you.

*

You cast a shadow of yourself
on those you love.

*

I searched the stardust in your eyes
for a recognition of me.
Unsaid words burn on my tongue.

*

in this darkness, things
that truly matter - shine
just watch, with curious eyes,
everything falls in its place.
you are a part of me
and I am a part of you
swimming the endless sea
we are in cosmos
and cosmos is in us

*

the broken pieces of me
recognize and sympathies
with the broken pieces of you

*

Hope & fear are the same boat,
leading from wanting to worrying.
Your mind is a sailor,
let it find its magic,
sailing through the
enraged storms.

*

you give love
but you run away
unable to receive it

*

you should know,
there is no failure
is you don't succeed
in the what you set out for yourself
you can always start again.

*

Mind gathering thoughts from the surrounding.
Screaming all day long, dragging you with it.
Takes years of intentionally searching for your own truest
voice.

*

Thoughts are colours,
your mind the painter,
and your life a canvas.

*

Everyone is suffering,
some just hide it more.
It's okay to take your time
and heal, you're not supposed to be
running around open wounded

*

When you're making memories
You're also making history

*

Her skin is a shield, yet somehow he managed to reach inside
her heart, with warmth in his eyes and kindness in his voice.
They are walking their own path, yet they cross here and there,
as if they are leading in the same direction. It feels as if it's just
one long journey back to themselves.
They know each other's souls.
She asks into the blank darkness of the night:
"Do I reside in a corner
of your heart?" There is no reply, just a shiver
running through her body.
He is close by.

*

I admit to being called soft,
as if it's a weakness.
They fail to see the strength,
They fail to see the depth
of emotions, that rage inside,
for they themselves have numbed the heart;
we do our best to survive.
But my softness has taught me the beauty of life,
It has taught me to listen and feel it all,
it has taught me to pass it on.
For why do we hide the things
that should be released?

*

You are like a rose bud in my bosom,
springing from my rib cage.
I hold you tenderly, guarding from the frost.
I keep on believing you will grow
and I'll get to see you blossom.

*

My hand over your chest
Calming your restless nights
Find the light in the darkness,
dear one.

*

We dress and undress

several times a day.
Wearing our roles,
getting lost along the road.
Which one we actually are
- at the heart?

*

In me is an insatiable hunger
for adventure, to rejoice in wide open spaces,
yet I'm caught like a boat tied up in a harbour.

*

You will come to realise that a safe place
was never a place, but a person.

About the Author

Writing down poems somewhere between mothering and working as a midwife. There's always that voice inside that yearns to write things down. Using pen name Natašek.

Author of Colours of the sea and Endless space between.

Read more at https://natasek.blogspot.com/.